Eduardo's List

Janice Marriott
illustrated by Nina Price

The phone rings.
"Hi, Eduardo. Are you coming to the game?" asks Carlos.

"Yes," says Eduardo.

"Don't forget," says Carlos. "Write it down. It's at 6 p.m. tonight, Friday."

"OK. I've written it down. Cool. Bye."

The phone rings.
"Hi, Eduardo. Are you coming to the pool?" asks José.

"Yes," says Eduardo.

"Don't forget it," says José.
"Make a note. It's at 10 a.m. tomorrow, Saturday."

"OK. I've made a note. Cool. Bye."

The phone rings.
"Hi, Eduardo. Are you coming to see me?" asks Dad.
"Yes," says Eduardo.

"Don't forget," says Dad. "Jot it down. It's for lunch tomorrow, Saturday, at 1 p.m."

"OK. I've jotted it down. See you tomorrow. Bye."

Eduardo reads his list.
The phone rings.
"Hi, Eduardo. Are you coming to the mall?" asks Samuel.

"When?" asks Eduardo.

"Remember, we talked about it," says Samuel. "Scribble it down. I'll meet you at 10 a.m. on Sunday. I'll see you at the music store."

"OK. I've scribbled it down. Bye."

Eduardo reads his list again.
He looks at the clock.
It's 5 p.m. He'd better go!

"Where are you going?" asks Mom
as he opens the door.
"Come back and do your homework!"

"But, Mom, I'll be late!"
Eduardo groans.

"Now," says Mom.

He takes his homework notebook out.
He reads, "For homework on Friday, make a list."

"Cool!" he shouts.

"Mom, I've done my homework. I've made a list!"

"Where are you going?" Mom asks
as Eduardo races out the door.

"It's all on my list," Eduardo says.
"My list tells you where I'm
going to be,
when I'm going to be there,
and who I'm going to be with!"

He runs down the steps.

Mom looks at the list.
"Cool," she says.